BITCOIN MINING

Bitcoin and Cryptocurrency Mining

By Sam Sutton

~~~

BITCOIN

Mastering Bitcoin for Starters

By Sam Sutton
~~~

© Copyright 2018 By Sam Sutton
All Rights Reserved

The transmission, duplication or reproduction of any of the following work including specific information will be considered an illegal act irrespective of if it is done electronically or in print. This extends to creating a secondary or tertiary copy of the work or a recorded copy and is only allowed with express written consent from the Publisher. All additional right reserved.

The information in the following pages is broadly considered to be a truthful and accurate account of facts and as such any inattention, use or misuse of the information in question by the reader will render any resulting actions solely under their purview. There are no scenarios in which the publisher or the original author of this work can be in any fashion deemed liable for any hardship or damages that may befall them after undertaking information described herein. This book should not be taken as financial or investment advice, and the author does not take any responsibility for inaccuracies, omissions, or errors which may be found therein.

Additionally, the information in the following pages is intended only for informational purposes and should thus be thought of as universal. As befitting its nature, it is presented without assurance regarding its prolonged validity or interim quality. Trademarks that are mentioned are done without written consent and can in no way be considered an endorsement from the trademark holder.

The contents of this book are intended to convey general information only. You should not treat any information herein as a call to make any particular decision regarding cryptocurrency usage, legal matters, investments, taxes, cryptocurrency mining, exchange usage, wallet usage, etc. It is strongly suggested that you seek advice from your own financial, investment, tax, or legal adviser. This book should not be taken as financial or investment advice, and the author does not take any responsibility for inaccuracies, omissions, or errors. The author of this work is not responsible for any loss, damage, or inconvenience caused as a result of reliance on information as published on, or linked to, this book.

The author of this book has taken careful measures to share vital information about the subject. May its readers acquire the right knowledge, wisdom, inspiration, and succeed.

TABLE OF CONTENTS

Introduction 7

Chapter 1: What is Bitcoin? 9

Chapter 2: Getting Started with Bitcoin 17

Chapter 3: Understanding Blockchain and
Bitcoin Transactions 19

Chapter 4: Where to Keep Your Bitcoin 23

Chapter 5: Buying Bitcoin 27

Chapter 6: Using Bitcoin 31

Chapter 7: Investing in Bitcoin 33

Chapter 8: Bitcoin for Business 39

Chapter 9: Bitcoin mining 41

Chapter 10: Security of Bitcoin 45

Conclusion 47

INTRODUCTION

Congratulations on downloading this book and thank you for doing so.

The following chapters will teach you the ins and outs of investing in bitcoin and how you can turn it into a goldmine of profits:

Chapter 1 lays down the basics to help you to have a good understanding of what bitcoin really is.

Chapter 2 gives an overview and teaches how you can get started with using bitcoin.

Chapter 3 discusses the blockchain technology which is the backbone technology of bitcoin. It also explains how a bitcoin transaction works.

Chapter 4 talks about the different types of bitcoin wallets.

Chapter 5 teaches how you can buy bitcoins.

Chapter 6 is about using bitcoin. Learn about receiving, sending, and receiving bitcoins.

Chapter 7 teaches effective strategies that you can use to invest in bitcoin.

Chapter 8 talks about businesses that use bitcoins, as well as how *you* can easily use it for your own business.

Chapter 9 is about bitcoin mining. Learn about the different ways to mine bitcoins.

Chapter 10 talks about the security of using bitcoin.

There are plenty of books on this subject on the market, thanks again for choosing this one! Every effort was made to ensure it is full of as much useful information as possible. Please enjoy!

CHAPTER 1:
WHAT IS BITCOIN?

Bitcoin is undeniably the number one cryptocurrency in the world. What is a *cryptocurrency*? A cryptocurrency is a kind of digital asset that is held electronically. It is stored online; and therefore, it does not have a physical existence. Just like other cryptocurrencies, bitcoin functions as a substitute for money.

Bitcoin is a *decentralized* digital currency. It is decentralized in the sense that there is no government, organization, group, or person that exercises authority over it. This makes it free from any and all forms of manipulation and undue advantage. This is also why so many people trust bitcoin.

It should be noted that although cryptocurrencies like bitcoin work as a substitute for money, they are not considered as fiat money or legal tender. Fiat money refers to the established and official currency of a state such as the US dollar. Legal tender refers to "that which a debtor may compel a creditor to accept payment." Although bitcoin is not considered as fiat money or legal tender, it is noteworthy that many individuals and merchants these days now accept bitcoin as a medium of payment. In fact, among all the cryptocurrencies out there, bitcoin is the most accepted cryptocurrency. Just to give you an idea, the giant computer company, Microsoft, now accepts payments in bitcoins. Not only that, Virgin Galactic, a huge company engaged in space tourism, also accepts payments in bitcoins. Other known companies like Overstock, Fiverr, Steam, Peach Airlines, Lionsgate Films, and Stripe, among many others, accept and use bitcoins. As Bitcoin gets more and more popular in the market, the more people and businesses start to use it.

Brief History

In 2008, a paper was posted on a cryptography mailing list. It was entitled *Bitcoin: A Peer-to-Peer Electronic Cash System*. It was published under the name Satoshi Nakamoto, which turned out to be just a pseudonym. The following year, Bitcoin was finally launched in the market. It came into existence just after Nakamoto himself mined the very first bitcoin block known as the *genesis block*.

Back then, bitcoin did not have any significant value. In fact, so many people did not even realize how much bitcoin would grow. At that time, it was the members of the cryptocurrency community themselves who decided how much bitcoin would worth. For example, there was a famous transaction where two pizzas where bought for 10,000 bitcoins. This is still posted on the *bitcointalk* forum. As you can see, most of the people there did not take it seriously. If only they knew how much bitcoin would develop. As of January 16, 2018, the price of 1 bitcoin is around 13,500 USD.

Who is Satoshi Nakamoto?

When people talk about the creator of bitcoin, they are well aware that it was made by Satoshi Nakamoto. But, who exactly is Satoshi Nakamoto? The truth is that up to the present time, nobody knows the real identity of Satoshi Nakamoto. There are many different views about this: There are those who say that Nakamoto is actually composed of a group of computer experts and programmers, while others say that Nakamoto is even a woman. Another theory is that Satoshi Nakamoto is Hal Finney, the man who first downloaded the bitcoin software and received 10 bitcoins from Nakamoto simply for downloading it. However, when Mr. Finney was still alive, he had already denied this claim. It is also worth mentioning that *Satoshi* is also the smallest unit of bitcoin. Bitcoin has 8 decimal places. Example: 0.00000001 = 1 satoshi. Simply put, no one knows for certain the true identity of Satoshi Nakamoto. Nakamoto has long withdrawn from the public that nobody even knows his whereabouts. However, even though nobody knows who the real Satoshi Nakamoto is, and even if his identity remains a mystery forever, the fruit of his labor and contribution to the world, bitcoin, has gained worldwide popularity and success.

Why Invest in Bitcoin?

It is not a secret that most people who engage in the cryptocurrency market and possess bitcoins do not really use such cryptocurrency as a mere medium of exchange. In fact, they view bitcoin as a form of investment. So, you must be thinking: *Just how much profit can I reasonably make?* To give you an idea, here is the classic example: If you had invested even just $500 in bitcoin in 2009 or even in 2010, then you would have already earned millions by now. Yes, this is how profitable investing in bitcoin can be. Unlike investing in stocks where an annual return of 30% is already considered very high, you can obviously earn so much more when you invest in bitcoin. Hence, many professional stock investors have started moving their investments from stocks into bitcoins. Another benefit of investing in bitcoin is that you do not have to wait for a year just to experience a significant price increase. It is not uncommon for the price of bitcoin to increase by more than 30% within a week. There was even a time when the price of bitcoin increased by $2,000 in just a week's time.

Investing in bitcoin is also easy and convenient. Since cryptocurrencies are held electronically online, all you need is Internet access to start investing, and you can manage your account and all your investments in the comfort of your home. In fact, you can even do all these directly from your mobile phone. Indeed, now is the time for you to enjoy the beauty of technology and the profitability of bitcoin.

Of course, just like any other investment, there is also a risk that you may not earn anything and that you may even lose your investment. However, there are strategies that you can do to prevent this from happening. By using the right strategies as revealed in this book, you can effectively increase your rate of success by more than 75%.

So, should you invest in bitcoin? Well, if you are the type who is afraid of taking risks, then perhaps this investment is not right for you. However, if you are the type who wants to earn and enjoy a high amount of profit, if you are willing to take risks and spend time and effort to study the market, if you want a proven way to achieve financial freedom, then investing in bitcoin might just be the best investment decision that you can ever make.

High Volatility

When people talk about bitcoin, they usually say that it has a high volatility. This is true. But, what does it mean when you say that bitcoin has a *high volatility*? This means that the price of bitcoin changes rapidly and significantly. This explains why it is possible for you to earn more than 200% profit in just a few days. However, be careful about this since this also implies that it is also possible for the price of bitcoin to drop just as fast. This is a normal part of the risk of investing in bitcoin or any other cryptocurrency. The whole cryptocurrency market itself is simply highly volatile. However, do not let this discourage you. Just remember that it is exactly this high volatility nature of bitcoin that makes it a highly lucrative investment. The good news is that if you study the past and current trend of bitcoin, you can easily see that it is a very profitable investment. Indeed, the price of bitcoin as of the beginning of 2018 has been gradually decreasing. However, keep in mind that it first increased significantly. This is merely part of the usual fluctuations that you can expect in the market. The important thing is that, in the long run, the value of your investment should be growing. Bitcoin has well established itself for years, and nobody can deny that it is still the number one and most successful cryptocurrency in the market.

Be careful with your understanding of high volatility. Many people think that high volatility means that after a significant price increase, then the price will drop significantly afterward, and vice versa, as if it balancing the rise and fall of the price on its own. This is a wrong understanding of high volatility. Take note that bitcoin (as well as other cryptocurrencies) does not balance itself on its own. Instead, some factors affect its price, such as market competition, economy, technological developments, market acceptance, and government regulations, among many others. Hence, you need to consider all these factors when predicting whether the price of bitcoin will rise or fall, but rest assured that a cryptocurrency will not balance its price movements all by itself. This is also why you need to do research and analysis when you engage in the cryptocurrency market.

What are Altcoins?

When you read about bitcoin, you will definitely also encounter other cryptocurrencies like Ethereum, Litecoin, Ripple, Lisk, OmiseGO, and others. All of these are altcoins. Simply put, all cryptocurrencies are considered as altcoin except bitcoin. Bitcoin has established itself strongly in the market that it has become the leading standard of all cryptocurrencies, such that all other coins are merely called as *altcoins*, a term that is simply short for *alternative coins*. To date, there are already more than 1,000 altcoins that have been created. Still, among all the cryptocurrencies in the world, Bitcoin holds the number one position and is considered the top and most successful and popular cryptocurrency of all.

Anonymity

Bitcoin users enjoy a certain level of anonymity. This is because, in a bitcoin transaction, no personal details will be revealed. This is true even though bitcoin has a *public* blockchain. When you look at the bitcoin blockchain, you will only see a bitcoin wallet address of the sender and of the bitcoin wallet address of the recipient. You will also see the amount of bitcoins involved in the transaction, as well as a time stamp. However, the names and other sensitive information will remain confidential. What about the bitcoin wallet address? It is simply like a long string of random letters and numbers, and a bitcoin user can always request for a new wallet address for free with just a few clicks of a mouse. In fact, it is suggested that to minimize exposure, you should request for a new wallet address for every new transaction that you make.

On legal matters

Although bitcoin is decentralized in such a way that no central authority governs and controls it, it does not mean that states do not have the power to regulate its use within their jurisdiction. Due to the level of anonymity enjoyed by bitcoin users, it is not hard to understand why some states like Ecuador and Bolivia completely outlaw the use of bitcoins, as well as all other cryptocurrencies. Due to the nature of cryptocurrencies, they can easily be used in illegal activities like money laundering and tax evasion. The good news is that in many countries like in the U.S., Canada, Europe, Russia, South Korea, Singapore, Philippines, and so many others, the use of bitcoins and other cryptocurrencies is legal. Russia used to consider it as illegal but then it changed its position in 2017 and now also uses bitcoin. Over time, more and more states and businesses are being open to the use of bitcoin.

As a bitcoin investor, you should keep an eye on the latest government regulations on bitcoin and other cryptocurrencies. Although there are states that do not outlaw the use of bitcoin in their territories, it does not mean that they can no longer impose regulations on the use of bitcoin. As of recently, the price of bitcoin and other known cryptocurrencies have been experiencing a decline. According to the news, this is because of certain regulations imposed by various states. But, do not worry; this has always been expected to happen. This is just one of the fluctuations that you can expect in the market. Soon enough, things will get more stable, and you can expect the prices to increase again. One thing to remember is that legal matters, especially the regulations imposed by states, have a strong influence on the price of bitcoin, as well as other cryptocurrencies. For example, when a news piece was released stating that South Korea was considering shutting down all its cryptocurrency exchanges, the price of bitcoin and all other cryptocurrencies experienced a significant decrease in price. This is nothing new; back in 2017, China also made a similar declaration, and the price of bitcoin and altcoins also experienced a drop in price. Once again, the lesson here is to consider how governments react to the use of cryptocurrencies, especially with regard to their legalities.

CHAPTER 2:
GETTING STARTED WITH BITCOIN

Now that you have a good idea of what bitcoin is, it is time for you to have an overview of how to get started with bitcoin so that you will know just what to expect. Well, the first step is to create a bitcoin wallet. There are basically just two types of bitcoin wallets: The hot and cold wallet. However, they are further divided into more specific types. Do not worry; they will be discussed in detail later on in this book. For now, you should learn what hot and cold wallets are.

Simply put, a hot wallet is a kind of bitcoin wallet that is stored completely online. As such, it is very easy and convenient to use. Hence, most cryptocurrency users use a hot wallet. All that you need to do is to sign up for an account for free from a wallet provider like *Coinbase*. The signing up process usually takes less than two minutes to complete. After which, you can now start using your bitcoin wallet. A cold wallet is the kind of bitcoin wallet where you store your private and public keys *offline*. Hence, to access your wallet and transfer funds, you will need to have your cold wallet in your possession. This is an added and highly effective security measure.

The next step is for you to own bitcoins. After all, the only way to invest and take advantage of bitcoin is by having bitcoins of your own. Although there are different ways to earn bitcoins, the quickest and fastest way to earn a good amount of bitcoins is by buying them. Bitcoin wallets like Coinbase will allow you to buy (and even sell) bitcoins directly from the wallet itself. This makes things very convenient for you. However, if the wallet that you use does not allow you to buy bitcoins, then you can simply sign up for a trading account with a cryptocurrency trading broker.

Again, creating an account is also fast and simple. However, it is important that you only work with a reliable and trusted broker. When you search online, you will surely find different brokers. As an investor, it is important that you only work with a reliable broker, so be sure to check the latest ratings and reviews of a broker prior to making any form of deposit.

Once you have bitcoins of your own, then you can keep them, and then sell them at a profit once they appreciate in value. However, the activity of investing in bitcoin is much more technical than just buying and selling bitcoin. After all, how do you know the right time to buy and sell bitcoin? Do not worry; all these will be discussed later in the book. For now, it is important for you to just have an idea of how you will get started.

As a bitcoin investor, you should know that research and analysis should be part of your day-to-day activity as an investor. Hence, before you even start to actually use and invest in bitcoin, you should already begin reading about the cryptocurrency market by now. Take note that bitcoin has many other competitors. Therefore, even though you may only intend to invest in bitcoin, it is still important that you keep an eye on its competitors, such as Ethereum, Litecoin, Ripple, Dash, and others. And, who knows, you might even be able to discover other profitable investment opportunities in the process.

CHAPTER 3:

UNDERSTANDING BLOCKCHAIN AND BITCOIN TRANSACTIONS

Before we discuss the specific steps on how you can profit by investing in bitcoin, you should first understand the technology behind bitcoin. Take note that the backbone technology of bitcoin is known as the *blockchain technology* or simply *blockchain*. What is blockchain? It is a public and decentralized distributed ledger which also acts as a repository of all transactions. It is made of records referred to as blocks. Before any block is added to the chain, it will undergo a strict process of verification and confirmation, which ensures that all the records that will be added to the chain are true and correct. Every new block is connected to the block that comes before it using what is known as a *hash pointer*. This way, all of the blocks in the blockchain network are interconnected with one another.

The blockchain is decentralized, which means that no organization exercises authority over it. It functions on its own free from any and all forms of influence and manipulation. This is why many people trust this system since there is no need for human intervention and control. The blockchain is also public, which means that all of the transactions are viewable to everyone on the network. This gives it added transparency and fairness and ensures that all transactions are legitimate and correct.

The blockchain technology is also an effective preventive measure against double spending and fraud, which are common problems in financial circles. When you use blockchain, there is absolutely no way to withdraw, modify, or cancel a transaction after it is confirmed. Not even Satoshi Nakamoto himself can stop or change it.

It also has a high level of security. Keep in mind that the blockchain network is spread over a wide connection of computers. For an attack against the blockchain system to be successful, the said attack has to possess at least 51% of the total hash rate of the entire bitcoin blockchain. Since the network is spread over a vast number of computers, achieving the said 51% can be considered as impossible. Take note that an attack with less than 51% hash rate is still possible, but you simply cannot expect for it to be successful. This is the idea behind the 51% attack concept.

It is noteworthy that bitcoin is not the only one that is gaining lots of attention and popularity. The blockchain technology has been making a name for itself apart from it being associated with bitcoin and other cryptocurrencies. This is because the blockchain has many other possible applications that are even well beyond the financial sector. Still, it can be said that blockchain is still a fairly new and young technology. Hence, there is still a room for improvement, and it is definitely something to keep an eye on.

How a Bitcoin Transaction Works

Every bitcoin transaction goes through a process. You should remember that there are 3 parts of a bitcoin transaction: Input, Output, and the Amount. Let us take a look at them one by one:

✓ Input

Let us say that person A wants to send 2 bitcoins to person B. Before person A can send B 2 bitcoins, it is only logical that person A must first have 2 bitcoins in his wallet. This is what is referred to as the *input*. Simply put, it refers to the bitcoins in the sender's wallet, the amount of which should be greater than or at least equal to the amount that he wants to send to another.

✓ Output

The output refers to the receiver. In our example, it is person B. More specifically, it refers to the *wallet address* of person B. Take note that in a bitcoin transaction, you do not send the bitcoin directly to the name of the receiver. In a blockchain, the transfer of bitcoins is made between wallet addresses. Hence, if you are the sender, then you should first ask for the bitcoin wallet address of the receiver. It is to this wallet address where you will send bitcoins.

✓ Amount

Obviously, this refers to the amount that is involved in a transaction. In this case, the amount is 2 bitcoins.

What about mining?

Mining refers to the process of verifying, confirming, and adding blocks or records to the blockchain. In a bitcoin transaction, once miners confirm a transaction, it can no longer be canceled, withdrawn, or modified. As you can see, mining is an important part of the blockchain ecosystem. Without mining, no new block or record can be added to the blockchain. Hence, in a bitcoin blockchain, you can rest assured that there is always a demand for miners.

CHAPTER 4:
WHERE TO KEEP YOUR BITCOIN

Now, let us move on to the more practical side: Do you keep or store your bitcoins? Remember that there are two kinds of bitcoin wallets: the hot and cold wallet. Now, these two main categories of bitcoin wallets are further classified into several specific types. You need to understand their differences so that you will know which wallet type will best suit your needs. Let us look at them one by one:

- *Online Wallet*

An online wallet is the most common type of bitcoin wallet. It is also known as a *web wallet*. This is the most commonly used type of bitcoin wallet as it is very easy and convenient to use. Good examples of an online wallet are Coinbase and GreenAddress. This is the type of wallet that you can easily access and manage simply by going online and logging in to your wallet through the site provided by your wallet provider. However, take note that this is a hot wallet, so you cannot expect for it to be a secured as a cold wallet. The good news is that many of the reputable hot wallets have already updated their security features. But, if security is your main concern, then a cold wallet is still the best choice.

- *Mobile Wallet*

A mobile wallet is another type of hot wallet. It is also an online wallet; but this time, you should download the wallet application on your mobile phone. Normally, you can download the application for free at the Apple and/or GooglePlay store. Many people use their phones to access the Internet, so having a mobile version of your wallet can be really handy at times. Do not worry; many web wallets like GreenAddress and Coinbase also have a mobile version of their bitcoin wallet.

• *Desktop Wallet*

A desktop wallet is a type of cold wallet. When you use a desktop wallet, you will store your public and private keys on a computer, which may also be a laptop computer. Before you use any computer as a desktop wallet, you should first reformat your computer or at least ensure that it is free from any malware and virus. Also, once you start using a computer as a cold wallet, you should no longer connect it to the Internet. This is what makes a cold wallet more secure than a hot wallet. Once something is exposed to the Internet, then it gets exposed to online hazards like hackers, attackers, and viruses. Since cold wallets are held offline, they are free from such risks. This is what makes a desktop wallet and other cold wallets very secured.

• *Hardware Wallet*

A hardware wallet functions just like a desktop wallet. But, instead of storing your public and private keys in a computer, you get to store them in a hardware. Although you can use an ordinary USB for this purpose, such is not advisable since an ordinary USB does not have enough protective features and can get easily get corrupted. Different kinds of hardware wallets are sold in the market specially made for this purpose, such as the Ledger Nano. However, they can get expensive. The good news is that to date, there has been no report or issue of any hardware wallet getting hacked or compromised. Hence, this is definitely one of the best bitcoin wallets that you can use in terms of having a very high level of security.

- *Paper Wallet*

A paper wallet is another famous type of cold wallet. When you use a paper wallet, you get to store your private and public keys on a paper. You can print them on paper. Ideally, you should keep several copies. Needless to say, you should store them in a safe place where they will not be stolen. Take note that although cold wallets offer high security, this is only as far as online hazards are concerned. They still cannot protect you from thieves or from losing or breaking your cold wallet.

Which wallet type should you use?

When choosing the right wallet for you, you need to strike a balance between security and convenience. For convenience, then any of the hot wallets would be a good choice. If you want to focus more on security, then you should use a cold wallet.

When choosing a wallet, you should think about how you intend to use your bitcoins. If you know that you will most likely transact with bitcoins on a regular basis, then you should use a hot wallet. However, if you just want to make a long-term investment where you just want to keep your bitcoins for a period of time, then using a cold wallet would be a better choice.

You are also free to use several wallet types at the same time. Hence, you can have a cold wallet and a hot wallet at the same time. You can use a hot wallet for short-term investments and for your day-to-day transactions, and then you can use a cold wallet at the same time for your long-term investment in bitcoin. There are also professional bitcoin investors who use multiple hot and cold wallets at the same time. You may find this necessary once you have a high number of bitcoins. After all, it is not advisable to keep all your bitcoins in a single wallet despite how secured you believe it to be. As they say, "Do not put all your eggs in one basket." The same is true when it comes to storing and keeping your bitcoins.

CHAPTER 5:
BUYING BITCOIN

How do you buy bitcoins? Buying bitcoins is easy. In fact, there are hot wallets like Coinbase and coins.ph will allow you to purchase bitcoins directly from the wallet itself. Now, if this is not possible, then you can sign up for a trading account with a cryptocurrency trading broker. There are brokers like eToro that will allow you to deposit fiat money and buy bitcoins on the trading platform itself. You may also want to use *localbitcoins*. It is like a marketplace where people buy and sell bitcoins. However, you need to be cautious when you use such kind of cryptocurrency marketplace as there are many scammers out there. Another popular option is to buy bitcoins using PayPal by through Virwox. However, take note that this is not a suggested approach as the cost can get very expensive. Hence, there are only two suggested ways to buy bitcoins: Through your bitcoin wallet and a trustworthy cryptocurrency trading broker.

Buy price vs. Sell price

Before you purchase bitcoins, you first need to understand that there is a difference between the buy price and the sell price. The buy price is always higher than the sell price. This difference in price is how a broker or seller makes a profit. This also means that right after you buy bitcoins, you cannot just sell them immediately after their price fluctuates a little higher as you will most probably end up with a loss since the sell price will be lower than the price at which you bought your bitcoins. Be sure to keep this in mind both when selling and buying bitcoins.

Check the market price

Before you buy and sell bitcoins, be sure to check its current price in the market. Do not forget that the price of Bitcoin fluctuates rapidly. This is to ensure that you are buying/selling your bitcoins at a fair price. A good way to do this is to visit the site of well-known cryptocurrency traders like Bitfinex, Binance, and Bittrex. You can also check well-established websites that share information about the cryptocurrency market, such as *coinmarketcap* and *coingecko*.

Timing

Do not just buy bitcoins right away. Before you make a purchase, you should first study the cryptocurrency market. Do not forget that bitcoin has a high volatility and that its price continuously changes. You definitely would not want to buy bitcoin when its price is falling down. Therefore, it is important that you study the market and use proper timing. Take note that the price of bitcoin rises and falls; hence, you may have to enter (buy) and leave (sell) the market every now and then, depending on the circumstances. By taking the effort to study the market, you will be able to save yourself some money and even lower your expenses and losses. Keep in mind that you do not just enter the market at any time you want. You need to be objective about it, and only buy bitcoins if you think that now is the moment to make a profitable investment. It is not uncommon for professional investors to wait for a day or even a week before they purchase bitcoins, even though they are eager to invest. Once again, proper timing is important when buying, as well as when selling bitcoins.

When selling bitcoins, you would want to sell them when their price is about to fall. However, this may also depend on your strategy. If you are making a long-term investment, then you should expect to face various price fluctuations in the market, and this includes facing some price decreases. Do not worry; in a long-term investment, the only important thing is to be at a profit once you close your position (when you sell your bitcoins). Hence, even if the price falls by 30% after two weeks, it would not matter if you can profit, say, by 100% the following week or so. Of course, you would not be investing blindly. To turn the odds in your favor and significantly increase your chances of making a profit, you will have to use effective strategies (as discussed later in this book).

CHAPTER 6:
USING BITCOIN

Using bitcoin is very easy and convenient. As we have already discussed, many merchants accept payments in bitcoin. Today, there are also many people around the world who use bitcoins for remittance or for sending funds to people located in another country. Since the use of bitcoin effectively cuts away the middleman like banks, it is a good way to minimize your cost. Now let us discuss what you need to do when you use bitcoins:

✓ **Sending bitcoins**

If you are the one who will send bitcoins, then all you need to do is ask for the bitcoin wallet address of the person to whom you intend to send bitcoins. A bitcoin wallet address looks like a long string of random letters and numbers. Be sure to copy and paste it correctly. Do not forget that once a transaction is confirmed, there is no way that you can cancel, amend, withdraw it. Therefore, be very careful when sending bitcoins. Be sure that you send it to the correct bitcoin wallet address. To send bitcoins, just access your wallet, key in the amount that you want to send, and then paste the wallet address of the recipient, and just click *send*. This entire process can be completed in less than a minute. As you can see, it is very simple. The recipient will soon be notified in his wallet that there is a pending receivable. Once the transaction has passed through several confirmations, then he will be able to finally receive the bitcoins that you send to his account. This normally takes just a few minutes from the time of sending the bitcoins.

✓ **Receiving bitcoins**

If you are the recipient, then you simply have to give your bitcoin wallet address to the sender. Again, to avoid committing mistakes, you should simply copy and paste your wallet address when sharing it with the sender.

✓ Storing bitcoins

We have already discussed the different ways to store your bitcoins. Make sure to keep your bitcoin wallet safe and secured. There are certain strongly suggested practices that you should observe, such as using a strong password and allowing the two-factor authentication. Keep in mind that your bitcoin wallet password is your main line of defense against a hacker or anyone who would want to access your account without your consent. To have a strong password, you should combine both upper and lower case letter. You should also use numbers and symbols in your password. Last but not least, avoid simply using the minimum required a number of characters. Instead, use a long password of at least 15 characters long. Needless to say, do not use a password that other people can easily guess. The two-factor authenticator is another line of defense that your account has. When you enable it, a code will be sent to your phone when anyone tries to access your account. Normally, you will have to enter this code after entering your password. The code changes within a few seconds, so it is very hard to predict correctly. You may have to download Google Authenticator app to be able to view the code. Do not worry; you can easily download this application for free from the GooglePlay or Apple store. If you are using a cold wallet, be sure to keep it in a safe place where it will not be broken or stolen.

CHAPTER 7:
INVESTING IN BITCOIN

Investing in bitcoin follows the usual trader's maxim: Buy low, sell high. However, this is easier said than done. To be able to invest successfully in bitcoin, you need to use effective strategies. Here are some notable strategies that you should learn and practice:

» *Fundamental Analysis*

Fundamental analysis is probably the most important strategy that you should learn. It is also referred as the lifeblood of investment. When you use fundamental analysis, you should focus on the *basics* or the fundamentals that affect bitcoin. Therefore, you should follow on the news and be up-to-date with the latest developments. The key to using this strategy is to gather as much good-quality information as you can. As they say, "Knowledge is power." It is a basic rule in investing that the more that you know and understand a certain asset, the more likely that you will be able to predict its price movement in the market. The same applies when you invest in bitcoin or any other cryptocurrency. When you use fundamental analysis, you should research and analyze the news, economy, competition among the different cryptocurrencies, market acceptance, and the past and current trend of bitcoin, among many others. Indeed, fundamental analysis is probably the strategy that takes a lot of effort, but it is well worth it. In fact, if you are serious about being a professional bitcoin investor, then it is a must that you should learn and use fundamental analysis. After all, this strategy can easily be incorporated even when you are using another strategy.

It is also strongly suggested that you should join online groups and forums about bitcoin and other cryptocurrencies. This is a good way to gather more information. From time to time, you will definitely learn some interesting ideas and strategies from these groups and forums. Since you are investing in bitcoin, be sure to join and participate in the *bitcointalk* forum. If you do not want to participate, then at least read the posts and learn something from them. It is also worth mentioning that many cryptocurrency developers are active in such kind of forums and groups, and this can allow you to gain valuable information against the competitors of bitcoin. Indeed, if you are serious about making continuous profit y investing in bitcoin or any other cryptocurrency, fundamental analysis is the strategy that you should always use.

» *Technical Analysis*

Technical analysis is a favorite among many bitcoin investors. This strategy is good if you are more of a visual person who loves to study and analyze graphs. When you use technical analysis, you will be looking at graphs and charts that reflect the price movements of bitcoin. The idea behind this strategy is that all of the elements or factors that affect the price of bitcoin can be summed up and have their final effect on the price. Therefore, this goes to show that simply by dealing with the price movements of bitcoin, you also get to deal with the many factors and elements that affect bitcoin. Of course, the advantage of using this approach is that it is much simpler than fundamental analysis where you need to research, read, and analyze so many pieces of information and even involves computations (numbers).

When you use technical analysis, the key is to be able to identify and take advantage of patterns. Yes, patterns do exist. However, they also come and go. Therefore, do not expect to see a pattern every time that you look at a graph or chart. A common mistake is to force to see a pattern even when there is actually no pattern to be seen. So, if you do not see a pattern, accept that it is not there and do not force an investment.

Technical analysis is a good strategy for short-term investments, while fundamental analysis is usually the choice when it comes to making long-term investments. Still, technical analysis is something that you can easily incorporate regardless of the strategy that you are using. After all, you simply have to view a chart or graph. Your trading broker will usually provide you with such tools (charts) that you need. If you do not have a trading broker, then there are many websites online that you can visit to see the price movements of bitcoin (as well as other cryptocurrencies).

Although you can use and depend completely on technical analysis, real experts suggest that you should still make use of fundamental analysis. The problem with technical analysis is that it does not give you the reasons behind the price movements; hence, you can barely come up with an accurate prediction. The best way to use technical analysis is still to combine it with fundamental analysis. If you use both strategies together properly, you can significantly increase your chances of making a profitable investment.

» *Averaging Down*

This is a good strategy to use if you want to be able to make a high amount of profit from an investment. This will allow you to purchase bitcoin at a "bargain" price. Here is an example of how to use this strategy: Let us say, for example, that the current price of bitcoin is $10,000. The first step is to make a buy order at its current price. Hence, you should buy bitcoin at the said price of $10,000. Now, if the price of bitcoin increases, then you make a profit. However, if the price of bitcoin drops, say, down to $9,500, then you should make another buy order at the said lower amount of $9,500. Now, if the price decreases again, then you should make another buy order. The key is simply to keep buying it while its price in decreasing. Hence, you get to buy bitcoin at a "bargain."

Okay, so this may seem like as if you are merely purchasing a losing asset, but this is actually not the case. Just imagine how much you will profit once the price of bitcoin recovers and goes back to its original price (the price when you first used this strategy), or even higher. All the buy orders that you have made will experience a nice profit. This is also an excellent strategy to use to take advantage of the volatility of the market.

Although this strategy is very practical and effective, do not forget that it is still considered an aggressive strategy. Hence, you should be careful when you use this approach. The proper way of using this strategy is to research the market first. Only use this strategy if you think that the price of bitcoin will most likely increase in the near future. If after doing your research and analysis, there are good reasons to believe that the price of bitcoin will most likely increase, then that is the only time that you should use this strategy.

» *Quick Sell*

This strategy is a good way to earn small yet consistent profits. The key to using this strategy is not to be greedy and close your position before your risk of exposure gets high. Here is an example of how you should use this strategy. Let us assume that the price of bitcoin is worth $10,000. You make a buy order at its current price of $10,000. Now, if the price increases, say, up to $10,200, then you should make a sell order right away and enjoy the small return of profits. Again, this is a good way to take advantage of a volatile market.

Take note, however, that the sell price is much lower than the buy price. Be sure to check the prevailing rate and only sell your bitcoin if you can make a profit out of it.

When you use this strategy, you should first study the market, especially the current trend of bitcoin. The best time to apply this strategy is while the price of bitcoin is increasing. Enter the market when it is hot and leave it even when it still appears to be profitable. The longer that you hold your position, the greater is your exposure to risk. Do not forget that when you use this strategy, you should prioritize controlling your risk. Hence, be contented with a small profit, and then start over.

» *Wait It Out*

There are times when it can be difficult to invest in bitcoin. For example, as of the start of 2018, the price of bitcoin has been unstable. This does not mean that it is no longer a good investment. Rather, this only shows that it may not be a good time to invest in bitcoin at the moment. Again, this is part of the usual fluctuations that you can expect when you deal with any kind of cryptocurrency/ however, you can rest assured that this will soon change (which is part of the nature of the cryptocurrency market). So, do not be like the other investors who keep on investing even when the market is down. To minimize your risk and losses, you should only invest in bitcoin when it is profitable in the market. But, when you see that its price has constantly been falling for days and weeks, the best action would be to just be patient and keep watch. Soon, bitcoin will again be able to recover, and that is the time for you to invest as its price continues to increase.

Remember that no matter how eager you are to invest in bitcoin, you must be patient to wait for the right opportunity. The important thing is that you are ready to invest once that opportunity arises. Therefore, it is your job to continue to follow and study the market. Wait out the bad times and join the hot streaks. Pay close attention to the market.

» *Go with the Flow*

Bitcoin is not really that hard to predict. For example, when it was announced in the news that China would close down all its local cryptocurrency exchanges, bitcoin and altcoins experienced a drop in price. However, when the news featured that Russia started to legalize bitcoins, the price of bitcoin surged upwards. The same is true when bitcoin was featured on CNN showing just how profitable an investment it is. Again, when Singapore declared that it would not issue any restriction yet on bitcoin, the price of bitcoin also increased. As you can see, sometimes you just have to go with the flow, and you can easily make a profit. Bitcoin is not always hard to predict. In fact, most of the time, it is very easy to predict the direction that its price movement will take in the market.

When you go with the flow, it is still advised that you do your fundamental analysis to be sure that you are not being misdirected. Sometimes what you read online or see in the news can be deceiving, especially when there is a pump and dump scheme. What is a pump and dump scheme? This fraudulent scheme is nothing new. In fact, it has been used in the stock market for years and is now being used in the cryptocurrency market. In a pump and dump scheme, a group of people will promote a certain cryptocurrency using some form of promotional hype. Their objective is to draw as much as positive attention and interest as possible to drive the price of the promoted cryptocurrency higher. However, once its price increases as other investors continue to make investments thinking that it is a profitable cryptocurrency, the people behind the scheme will then sell the cryptocurrency being promoted at a nice profit. The final result is that those behind the scheme can make a good profit while the investors (victims of the scheme) will be holding a losing asset. Hence, for you not to fall victim to this scheme, be sure to do your own analysis of the market and do not just follow the flow without doing any research.

CHAPTER 8:
BITCOIN FOR BUSINESS

Businesses around the world also use Bitcoin. In fact, by using bitcoin in business, you can effectively cut down your cost as you would no longer need a middleman like banks and other financial sectors for sending and receiving money (cryptocurrency) to another. You have full control of everything. The process, as we have already discussed, is also very quick and simple. Indeed, many businesses use and accept bitcoins. Let us look at some of these known businesses that use bitcoin:

• *Microsoft*

Microsoft needs no introduction. This computer giant is known worldwide, and now it is also known for accepting payments in bitcoin when you buy from Windows or Xbox store.

• *Virgin Galactic*

This company engaged in space travel also accepts bitcoin. So, if you have lots of bitcoins in your possession, you can now buy your trip to space. The founder of Virgin Galactic openly admitted that he supports bitcoin cryptocurrency.

• *Wikipedia*

As you know, Wikipedia is a huge website where you can get tons of valuable information for free. Anyone who uses the Internet is familiar with Wikipedia. Well, although you can use Wikipedia for free, it is also known for accepting donations in bitcoin.

• *Tesla*

If you are interested in science and technology, perhaps you would also find it interesting to know that the company, Tesla, also uses and accepts payment in bitcoin. In fact, some of its inventions were funded using bitcoins.

• *Peach Airlines*

The Japanese airline known as Peach Airline also accepts payment in bitcoin. So, if you want to travel to another country and would love to pay for your airfare using bitcoins, you might want to buy your ticket from Peach Airlines

• *Steam*
Steam is a popular gaming platform with millions of registered and active users. You can now buy games and upgrades using bitcoins.

• *Overstock*

This company allows you to purchase big-ticket items. You can now buy products from Overstock using bitcoins. In fact, they have even partnered with a famous bitcoin wallet known as *Coinbase*.

Many other companies and businesses use and accept payments in bitcoin. Now, if you own a business, you can also take advantage of bitcoins by paying your employees in bitcoins. Just be sure to check if this is allowed in the laws of your country. Also, if your business normally involves sending and receiving funds, then you should really consider using bitcoins as it can effectively lower your expenses and will allow you to have complete control of the process. It is also good to use bitcoins if you are to send "money" to someone who is located in another country. The bitcoin system is open 24 hours a day every day; hence, you can easily send and receive bitcoins with just a few clicks of a mouse. If you are the recipient, then simply give your bitcoin wallet address to the sender, and just wait for him to send your bitcoins into your wallet.

CHAPTER 9:
BITCOIN MINING

Mining bitcoins is another investment that you might want to consider. As we have already discussed, there is always a demand for miners in the bitcoin blockchain; otherwise, there is no way for any record or transaction to be added to the chain and be completed. Now, there are different ways to mine bitcoins. Let us go over them one by one:

- *Computer mining*

This is the most basic way to mine for bitcoins. This is where you use your own computer for mining. You can do this by downloading GUIMiner and joining a mining pool. The suggested pool is the Slush's pool. However, this is only a good method to give you an experience of mining, but it is not a recommended method if you want to earn a decent amount of bitcoins. The reason is that a computer alone does not have sufficient hash power to mine a decent amount of bitcoins. You will most probably end up with more expenses on electricity than the actual amount of bitcoin that you could mine. Also, when you mine using your own computer, you will have to worry about overheating. Take note of this because this can break your computer's CPU. So, when it comes to earning a decent amount of bitcoins, this is not a recommended method. But, if you just want to experience how it feels like to mine bitcoins and earn a little, then this is a good start.

- *Hardware mining*

Since a computer alone is not enough to mine a decent amount of bitcoins due to its low mining power, you will have to use a mining hardware to increase your hash or mining power. There are websites online like Amazon and eBay where you can buy a mining hardware. It is noteworthy that even if you mine using a hardware, you still have to use your computer. Hence, you should still be careful about any overheating issues. You should follow a schedule that will allow your computer and mining hardware to cool down from time to time. In choosing a hardware, you should look at the mining power and also the electric consumption. It is not uncommon to find a strong mining hardware but then also consumes high electricity. You need to consider this to ensure that you will end up with a decent positive profit.

• *Could mining*

This seems to be the most famous method of mining bitcoins nowadays. With cloud mining, you no longer have to worry about any overheating issue. You do not even have to purchase any mining hardware. In fact, you do not even have to mine anything at all. Hence, you do not even have to use your computer. Instead, all that you need to do is to wait for the cloud mining company to send you bitcoins. You will usually receive your bitcoins every week or as soon as you meet the minimum threshold. Okay, this may sound too good to be true, so what is the catch? Of course, there is also a catch. After all, you cannot expect for any business to send you bitcoins every week just out of kindness. The catch is that you will first have to invest. This means that you must first pay a cloud mining company. Now, you have to be careful about this because there are many scammers online who simply want to rip you off of your money. Therefore, before you invest in any cloud mining company, you need to do your research, check the latest reviews given to the mining company, and learn as much as you can about the said company.

A usual offer may look something like this: Invest (or pay) 1 bitcoin and earn up to 0.035 bitcoins every week. Okay, so far this seems very ideal. You just have to make some simple computation, and you would already know when you can recover your investment, and then you can earn positive profits after that. However, this is not always the case. The problem is that the offer only shows the *expected* return and not the actual return of profits. This means that using the given example, you may receive less than 0.035 every week. Before you make any form of deposit or investment, you need to be sure that the terms and agreements of the contract are clear to you. In case of doubts, do not hesitate the customer support team, and they would be happy to assist you. Also, pay attention to the expiration date. There are cloud mining companies that only render the contract valid for a year — and so this means that you should be able to recover your investment and then earn profits within the same time period. Other cloud mining companies honor a lifetime validity of contract. Again, the best way to be sure about this is to read the contract and talk with the customer support team of the cloud mining company for clarifications.

CHAPTER 10:
SECURITY OF BITCOIN

So, is it safe and secure to use bitcoin? The answer is *yes*. Otherwise, companies would no longer be using it in business. Although there were reports in the past that certain bitcoin wallets had been hacked, it is worth noting that the security of both hot and cold wallets has already improved significantly. In fact, many professional investors these days only use a hot wallet or the trading account provided by their cryptocurrency trading broker. The point here is that in terms of security, you can rest assured that bitcoin has a high level of security. Also, do not forget the 51% attack concept. Today, bitcoin is well distributed over a very vast network of computers, so just imagine how much hash rate power an attacker needs to have to penetrate the bitcoin blockchain successfully.

As an investor, you no longer need to worry whether or not bitcoin is secure because it is. Your main concern is how to ensure the security of your bitcoin wallet. As we have already discussed, you may want to use a cold wallet for this purpose. If you are using a hot wallet, be sure to enhance the security of your wallet by using a strong password and also activate the two-factor authentication or any other security features that your wallet provider may offer.

Bitcoin is also a continuously evolving technology, so you can expect for its security features to get even stronger and more secure over time. The good news is that as far as security is concerned, it can now be said that bitcoin is very secure. Hence, so many individuals and known businesses are using it, and many are still eager to learn about it so that they can also take advantage of the benefits of using bitcoin. In fact, there are those who believe that bitcoin is even more secure than traditional banks. As bitcoin continues to grow and dominate the cryptocurrency market, you can expect for more developments and improvements to happen over time.

CONCLUSION

Thanks for making it through to the end of this book. We hope it was informative and able to provide you with all of the tools you need to achieve your goals whatever they may be.

The next step is to apply everything that you have learned and start earning serious profits. Unfortunately, many people still think that bitcoin is a bubble that is about to burst. Well, it is up to you whether or not you want to believe this heresy. However, as far as the truth is concerned, those who believe that bitcoin is just a bubble failed to make any profit from it, while those who have taken the risk and believe in bitcoin as a profitable investment can earn a high amount of profits, even their way to complete financial freedom.

Finally, if you found this book useful in anyway, a review on Amazon is always appreciated!

CRYPTOCURRENCY MINING

The Ultimate Guide to Understanding Bitcoin, Ethereum, and Litecoin Mining

By Sam Sutton

~~~

© Copyright 2018 By Sam Sutton
All Rights Reserved

The following eBook is reproduced below with the goal of providing information that is as accurate and as reliable as possible. Regardless, purchasing this eBook can be seen as consent to the fact that both the publisher and the author of this book are in no way experts on the topics discussed within, and that any recommendations or suggestions made herein are for entertainment purposes only. Professionals should be consulted as needed before undertaking any of the action endorsed herein.

This declaration is deemed fair and valid by both the American Bar Association and the Committee of Publishers Association and is legally binding throughout the United States.

Furthermore, the transmission, duplication or reproduction of any of the following work, including precise information, will be considered an illegal act, irrespective whether it is done electronically or in print. The legality extends to creating a secondary or tertiary copy of the work or a recorded copy and is only allowed with express written consent of the Publisher. All additional rights are reserved.

The information in the following pages is broadly considered to be a truthful and accurate account of facts, and as such any inattention, use or misuse of the information in question by the reader will render any resulting actions solely under their purview. There are no scenarios in which the publisher or the original author of this work can be in any fashion deemed liable for any hardship or damages that may befall them after undertaking information described herein.

Additionally, the information found on the following pages is intended for informational purposes only and should thus be considered, universal. As befitting its nature, the information presented is without assurance regarding its continued validity or interim quality. Trademarks that mentioned are done without written consent and can in no way be considered an endorsement from the trademark holder.

TABLE OF CONTENTS

Introduction 53

Bitcoin, Ethereum and Beyond: What is Cryptocurrency 55

What is Cryptocurrency Mining? 61

What Can You Mine? 65

Getting Your Hardware and Building Your Rig 73

Dump for Dollars, or Keep the Cryptocurrency 85

Future of Cryptocurrency 91

Conclusion 95

INTRODUCTION

Congratulations on downloading your personal copy of *Cryptocurrency Mining*. Thank you for doing so.

Welcome to the ultimate cryptocurrency mining guide. If you are a newcomer to the cryptocurrency world, and you're interested in mining, this is perfect for you. You might only be curious about the workings of cryptocurrencies, and this is a perfect primer.

There are a lot of online resources for cryptocurrencies, and many of them tend to be difficult to understand. They are filled to the brim with abbreviations, technical details, and jargon that a beginner may find it hard to decipher. The following chapters were written with beginners in mind. We've done our best to keep the technical jargon to a minimum.

In order to begin mining, reading this book is a good first step, but your research shouldn't stop here. As you start to build you mining rig, or computer, you need to do more research. There are a lot of individual parts that go into mining, so let's dive in.

There are plenty of books on this subject on the market, thanks again for choosing this one! Every effort was made to ensure it is full of as much useful information as possible. Please enjoy!

BITCOIN, ETHEREUM AND BEYOND: WHAT IS CRYPTOCURRENCY

Cryptocurrency is a virtual or digital currency that provides security for its users by using cryptography. This security feature makes it hard to counterfeit. It most endearing feature is it is organic by nature meaning it does not get issued by a central authority. This makes it immune to any manipulation or interference by the government.

Due to cryptocurrency's anonymous nature, it makes them targets for criminal activities like tax evasion and money laundering.

Bitcoin was the first cryptocurrency to catch the public's attention. Bitcoin was created in 2009 by either an individual or group that called themselves Satoshi Nakamoto. By September 2015, over 14.6 million Bitcoins were already in circulation. These Bitcoins have a market value of about $3.4 billion. The success of Bitcoin has resulted in more cryptocurrencies being created like PPCoin, Namecoin, and Litecoin.

Drawbacks and Benefits

It is easy to transfer money between two people with cryptocurrency. Transfers are expedited by using private and public keys to help with security. The transfers are completed with very low fees, and this lets users stay away from the large fees that many financial institutions and banks will charge to do wire transfers.

At the center of Bitcoin is its blockchain that it stores all the transactions on. Every Bitcoin transaction that has ever been done will be on this blockchain. This gives a data structure that could be exposed to threats from hackers. It can be copied on any computer that runs Bitcoin software. Most experts view blockchain as being important to technologies like crowdfunding and online voting. Cryptocurrencies can even help lower processing fees.

Since cryptocurrencies don't have a central repository and are virtual, the currency can disappear if your computer crashes and you don't have a copy of your total currency. The amount a cryptocurrency can be exchanged for a different currency fluctuates a lot because prices change due to demand and supply.

These cryptocurrencies are not immune to hacking. In the short time, Bitcoin has been around, it has had 40 thefts. A few of these thefts were valued at over one million dollars. Many die-hard fans think cryptocurrencies is a currency that will hold its value, expedites exchange, is easier to move than hard metals, and government and central banks can't touch it.

Satoshi

Satoshi is the smallest unit of Bitcoin currency. It gets its name from the creator of Bitcoin, Satoshi Nakamoto. Cryptocurrencies only exist in the virtual world, unlike physical currencies like the US dollar or the British pound. A cryptocurrency can be broken up into smaller units like the dollar is broken down into cents and a pound is broken down into pence.

Bitcoin

Bitcoin follows ideas that were written in a white paper by Satoshi Nakamoto. This person or group's identity has never been verified. With the offer of lower transaction fees and being operated by a decentralized authority, it is no wonder why Bitcoin has risen to fame. The market cap for every bitcoin that is in circulation is over $7 billion.

You cannot physically hold bitcoins. The balance is stored in a public ledger along with every Bitcoin transaction in the cloud. Each transaction gets verified by huge amounts of computing power. Governments or banks can't back or issue Bitcoins, and they aren't valued as a commodity. In spite of being a legal tender, Bitcoins has triggered the creation of other currencies known as Altcoins.

Bitcoin's balances are stored in private and public keys that are long strings of letters and numbers that are linked by a mathematical algorithm that encrypts them. The public key is equivalent to a bank account number. This is the address that is published to everyone and where other people can send Bitcoins. Private keys are equivalent to a PIN number and need to be kept a secret. It is only used to authorize Bitcoin transfers.

Satoshi Nakamoto

This entity is the pioneer of cryptocurrency. Satoshi Nakamoto is the biggest enigma in cryptocurrency. It is still not clear if it is a she, he, a person, or a group. What we do know is Satoshi Nakamoto published a paper in 2008 that started the creation of cryptocurrency.

Bitcoin Cash

This is a fork of the Bitcoin Classic that became known in August 2017. This cryptocurrency can increase the block size and allows more transactions to be processed.

Since it was launched, Bitcoin has faced pressure from members of its community about scalability. Its block size which is one megabyte or one million bytes was set in 210. It slows down processing time and limits Bitcoin's potential just when it was getting popular. The limit of block size was put into the code to prevent attacks on the network when its value was very low. The value of Bitcoin has gone up substantially, and its block size has gone up to 600 bytes. This creates a scenario where transaction times would cause delays due to more blocks reaching maximum capacity.

Digital Copy

This is a record of every Bitcoin transaction that has been confirmed and was sent to the peer to peer network. This is a security feature on the Bitcoin platform that was created to help with double spending.

With the rise of cryptocurrencies, it also created a problem called double spending. This happens when a user buys something from two sellers and uses the same Bitcoins. This would be like trying to buy apples from two different vendors but using the same money for each transaction. This just can't happen. To solve this problem, Bitcoin's creators made a process where every transaction gets copied into a ledger and is verified by many different Bitcoin miners that are distributed throughout the network.

Each transaction gets recorded into the blockchain then copied and stored digitally across various networks within the decentralized system. To keep users from spending the same money twice, digital copy makes sure each participant has an encrypted digital copy of everybody's holding. Miners will verify each transaction and add them to the ledgers. By having digital copies in the Bitcoin ledgers, it is impossible for the history of transactions to get compromised. Any user that tries to change a transaction within the ledger for their own gain will not be successful since they can only change their own digital copy. In order for a transaction to be changed in the ledger, the user needs to have access to everybody's copy. This would prove to be very futile.

Bitcoin Unlimited

This is an upgrade to Bitcoin Core that gives larger block sizes. It was created to improve transaction speeds. Several improvements to this software have been proposed. These upgrades focus on increasing how many transactions that the system can do by increasing the size of blocks or speeding up the process.

Blocks are files where the Bitcoin transactions are stored. Every time a block gets completed, it gets put into the blockchain. Blocks are limited in size to one megabyte. Bitcoin Unlimited wants to increase the block size. This means that companies and individuals give the computing power that is needed to keep the records of all the transactions.

Since Bitcoins isn't controlled by a central authority, decisions about upgrades are made through a consensus. Any person or organization that pushes a change forward and the other members didn't agree to it can cause a fork in Bitcoin. This means the network that is running Bitcoin will split. Having a consensus-driven approach could make it hard to tackle issues that Bitcoin faces.

Problems with forking are one reason why Bitcoin Unlimited isn't the new standard. Having larger blocks can result in miners who have larger processing units will be more powerful and profitable, while small miners could get pushed out entirely.

Litecoin

Litecoin was created in 2011. It is a different cryptocurrency that is modeled after Bitcoin. Litecoin's creator is Charlie Lee. He is a graduate of MIT and used to work at Google. Litecoin just like Bitcoin is an open source network that is decentralized. It is different than Bitcoin because it can create blocks faster and uses scrypt as proof of work.

Litecoin was created with the hope of being the left to Bitcoin's right. It has gained popularity since it was created. Litecoin is also a peer to peer network. Litecoin was created to improve on Bitcoin's shortcomings. It has earned support as well as liquidity and trade volume. Litecoin was designed to create more coins faster. Litecoin is considered second to Bitcoin, but Litecoins are easier to get and send.

Altcoin

These are all the different cryptocurrencies that have been created after Bitcoin. They say they are better than Bitcoin, but that is still to be seen. Many alternative coins are targeting the limits that Bitcoin has and creating newer versions. There are many varieties of Altcoins.

Most of the Altcoins are built on Bitcoin's framework and makes the peer-to-peer as well. Some offer more efficient and cheaper ways to send transactions. Even though many features of the Altcoins overlap, they are still very different from each other.

Even with all these competitors, Bitcoin is still the leader in the cryptocurrency pack. Newer versions are being launched. This offer changes in areas such as DNS resolution, proof of stake, privacy, transactions speed, and so much more. Some have gained popularity. Some are not as well knows. Some examples of Altcoins are Novacoin, Zetacoin, Feathercoin, Peercoin, Dogecoin, Litecoin, and others. Litecoin is Bitcoin's closest competitor.

WHAT IS CRYPTOCURRENCY MINING?

As stated earlier, cryptocurrency uses a technique called cryptography to process transactions. This is a process that converts legible information into uncrackable codes that helps keep track of transfers and purchases. For a simple definition, it is just entries in a database that nobody can change without going through specific protocol.

Cryptography used the element of computer science and mathematical theory and was created during World War II to transfer information and data securely. It is now being used to secure money, information, and communications online.

Cryptocurrencies run on blockchains that are shared ledgers and get duplicated many times over a network of computers. An updated document gets made and distributed to anyone who holds cryptocurrency.

Each transaction that gets made and the owner of every cryptocurrency gets recorded onto the blockchain. These blockchains are run by miners that use very powerful computers to verify the transactions. They have to update every time a transaction gets made to ensure the information is authentic. This assures every transaction is processed safely, properly, and securely.

Miners get paid by minted cryptocurrency as payment for their work. These will show up as fees from merchants or vendors.

Cryptocurrency's value goes up and down based on supply and demand. It does not have a fixed value. Seller and buyers agree on a certain value that is fair based on what cryptocurrency is trading for elsewhere.

Transaction fees that are associated with credit cards are eliminated since the transaction is peer to peer. The identities of the seller and buyer are never revealed. Every transaction is public to everybody on the blockchain network.

People can get cryptocurrencies through exchanges online or trade it for normal currencies.

Mining for cryptocurrency has two functions: releasing new currency and adding transactions on the blockchain. Every block that gets added by miners has to contain proof of work.

Miners have to have a computer with a special program that helps them compete with other miners to solve complicated math problems. This takes large amounts of computer resources. Miners attempt to solve a block at regular intervals. They need the transaction's data and use hash functions to solve it.

The hash value is a value of numbers that can identify data. Miners use computers to find hash values less than the target. Whatever miner cracks it first is the one who actually mined the block and will get a reward. The reward for a block sits at 12.5 Bitcoins.

Early on, cryptography enthusiasts were the miners. As Bitcoin gained popularity and its value increased, mining is now a business on its own. Many businesses and people have begun investing in hardware and warehouses.

As businesses jumped on board, they soon realized they couldn't compete. Miners have started opening pools and combining their resources to compete better.

One business, Bank of New York Mellon Corp., has been using a blockchain platform since 2016 to help with US Treasury bond settlements. The privacy of the platform has allowed it to remain out of the grasp of regulatory agencies. When a bank decides to let its clients use it commercially, regulatory agencies might get into the action.

A mining kit contains a fan, cabling, memory, power supply, a processor, and graphics cards. The cost for this is around $2,400 to $3,800 if bought through Amazon. The best hardware for mining is AntMiner S9, AntMiner S7, and Avalon6.

Normal GPUs are not strong enough, so miners are beginning to use ASICs or application specific integrated circuits. To help with this shortcoming, AMD and Nvidia are working on GPUs that might be used just for this purpose.

There are two companies that are dominating the mining hardware, and they are Bitmain and Canaan. Bitmain is located in Beijing. It mines and manufactures hardware.

Mining Pools

Most mining pools are located in China and do about 81 percent of the hash rate. For Nvidia and AMD that dominate the gaming chip market, turning their focus off of their main business might not be a good course of action.

These companies have to create GPUs that were designed exclusively for the sole purpose of mining. These GPUs are a threat to the ASIC chips that are manufactured in China.

Exchanges and governments are contemplating about the regulations of cryptocurrencies. After MtGox, a Tokyo based exchange collapsed in 2014, Japan has introduced laws to protect users. Introducing taxes like a tax on capital gain of Bitcoin sales might slow down the cryptocurrency industry.

WHAT CAN YOU MINE?

Mining for cryptocurrencies and Bitcoin is very popular these days. As more people start mining, it gets harder to mine any type of cryptocurrency successfully.

To maximize your hashing power, you need to mine the currency that offers the most profit. Don't try to mine the difficult algorithms such as Bitcoin, try some easier cryptocurrencies. Once you have successfully mined the currency, convert it into the currency of your choice. You can do with by using an online exchange and thus maximizing profits.

Here are the cryptocurrencies that lead the pack:

- Bitcoin: With today's economy, each transaction we do has to go through the credit card company or a bank. They take out a fee for the transaction, and we have to hope they don't mess up. This is where Bitcoin comes in. At the center of Bitcoin are mathematical problems. Miners have to solve these. When a solution is found, the miner is rewarded with Bitcoins. Bitcoins are mined using powerful graphics cards.

- Ethereum: This platform is designed for people who want to create decentralized applications. In recent months, Ethereum has become very valuable and makes it the best choice for miners who are just beginning. It allows peer-to-peer transfer and a blockchain. This blockchain comes with its own language. This lets people use it for all sorts of decentralized applications. It is secured by cryptography. Ethereum doesn't have an ASIC. This doesn't mean you won't be able to make money. If you have a mining GPU, you can mine about $1,400 per year.

- Litecoin: This is another decentralized cryptocurrency. There is only about 84 million in existence. It offers low fees and quick transaction times. You can sell and buy it from other people and exchanges. You can use it to buy pretty much anything. If you use Antminer, you could mine about $6,000 per year.

- Dash: This is the first cryptocurrency that acts like fiat currency. You keep complete control of your money. You have total privacy, and there is no way to track the transactions. Transactions are processed instantly. There are virtually no fees since you control the money. Dash is one of three currencies that are most profitable. By mining using a specified ASIC, you could mine about $1,000 per year.

- Monero: This cryptocurrency is interchangeable. It prides itself on the privacy it gives to its users. Its value is increasing steadily. Investing in Monero hardware just might be the way to go. If you mine using a specified GPU, you could mine $1,400 per year.

- Zcash: This cryptocurrency is based on Bitcoin's platform but has one main difference. Zcash offers its users the option of encrypting their own transactions. This essentially means that the transaction's amount, the recipient's address, and the sender's address is all hidden from the public. Most think Zcash is the future of keeping transactions anonymous. Normal GPUs are able to mine Zcash like GTX 1080. It can also mine for Decred. Zcash has put a cap on how many coins can be mined. Jump in now as only 21 million will ever be mined.

- ZenCash: This cryptocurrency was made for user privacy. Most call it the privacy coin. All transactions are off the grid. This makes them extremely secure. It allows you to send coins straight to a recipient's address. This would be a great cryptocurrency to learn how to mine.

How It Works

Cryptocurrency creates blocks from all transactions. These get put together and creates a blockchain. Every time a transaction is done, the blockchain gets updated.

Miners use a process where they take the information and use formulas to process it. The result is a string of numbers and letters that is shorter than the actual transaction. This is known as a hash.

Every hash is similar to the hash that gets used first. Because every hash is based on the one in front of it, the next one will confirm the other ones were legitimate.

To mine for blocks, miners use specific GPUs to find answers to questions. When they find the answer, they receive a certain amount of coins as a reward. Miners use header metadata throughout the hash function. Each currency has its own algorithms. Litecoin uses Scrypt. Every time a valid hash gets found, it goes through the network and becomes part of the public ledger.

You are not able to fake your work and cheat. This is why all cryptocurrencies require proof of work. Ethereum is trying to get rid of proof of work and use proof of stake. If the miner can validate their work, they get rewarded with cryptocurrency.

Importance of an Efficient and Powerful GPU

Think about all the information that has been provided and you can understand why a powerful GPU is needed. You will be able to mine coins more successfully if you have a powerful GPU.

Powerful graphics cards use huge amounts of electricity. You need to think about how important the card's efficiency is as well. It might be better to buy several cheaper GPUs that have higher hash/power ratio. It might give you better profits. A good example of this type of GPU is the GTX 1050 Ti.

Mining is getting harder every day, so it is critical to have an efficient GPU. Some will cost you more in electricity bill than they will give you in revenue.

Factors That Harm the Efficiency of a Computer

You are not able to use just any graphics card to mine. Here are some cards to consider:

MHash/s

This is equivalent to how many numbers the card can handle during mining. You will use more hashes if you rate is high. If the hash rate is low, you won't use as many. What exactly does that mean? Higher hash rate means quicker results.

MHash/j

This is the number of hashes that the card can handle per energy joule. As stated earlier, mining uses a huge amount of electricity. Your graphics card will need to mine enough coins in order for you to make a profit after your electricity bill has been paid.

A larger number shows your card is more energy efficient. If the card is energy efficient, then you are saving yourself some money.

MHash/s/$

This is a way to show the performance/price ratio of a card. If it has a high number, you will get more for the money. If a card uses a lot of electricity and has a low hash rate, you won't be creating a lot of revenue, if any.

You need to find a card that has a good balance of performance and price. Mining for cryptocurrencies like Ethereum, Litecoin, and Bitcoin takes a very powerful graphics card. It actually takes several graphics cards. You will also need a motherboard that has the same amount of slots as GPU cards.

Make sure you have the correct power supply. If your computer doesn't have the right amount of power, it isn't going to work correctly.

Is Mining Right For You?

Mining is a great idea. Go out and purchase a mining GPI and watch the money roll in. Right?

Actually, no.

There are large warehouses in different countries that have very low electricity bills. These warehouses are home to thousands of GPUs, and the cost is anywhere from thousands to millions of dollars.

With this huge setup, mining is very profitable, and investors are making huge amounts of money. When an individual is mining on a personal computer at home, they might never see a return on their investment.

You can still benefit from mining. Some do it as a hobby that gives them a little something for their time. Unless you do it on a huge scale, you aren't going to see a whole lot of profits. If you just want to own some cryptocurrency, just purchase some.

Trading Cryptocurrency for USD or Other Cryptocurrencies

You will need to exchange your preferred cryptocurrency for Bitcoins first. Here is how to do it:

1. Create an account in an online exchange like Binance.

2. After the account has been created, now you will need to buy your preferred currency's wallet address. This address gets used with your mining software. The currency you mine gets put into this wallet. From there, you are able to exchange if for Bitcoin and then USD. To do this Hover over the tab that says Funds. A drop-down menu should appear. Now click on deposits/withdrawals. Look for your cryptocurrency and click on deposit. When asked, click agree and move on. You will be sent to a page that will show your personal address. Copy the code and put the software in this address.

3. After you have deposited cryptocurrency into your exchange account, you can decide to change it for Bitcoin. Here is how to do this:

   Go to the exchange's homepage but clicking on the logo. Go to the BTC Markets and look for your cryptocurrency. When you have chosen your currency, you will see it in the search results. Click on it. In the sell box, you can exchange your currency for Bitcoin. If you need to convert all the currency you own into Bitcoin, just choose 100 percent.

4. Now, you will need to transfer your Bitcoins out of the exchange you are using into another one like Gemini or Coinbase. After it has been transferred, you can exchange Bitcoins for USD. Here is how to do it:

   Go back to the deposits/withdrawals page. You can now withdraw your acquired Bitcoins out of your Bitcoin wallet like this:

   Type in your Bitcoin address. Go to either Gemini or Coinbase (whichever one you used). When you have finished the registration, now click on accounts. Click receive under the BTC wallet. You should see a QR code pop up. This is your wallet's address. You will need to copy and paste this into the BTC withdrawal address. Choose your amount and then submit.

5. The final step is to sell you Bitcoin for normal currency. Go to the sell/buy tab and click on sell. Just choose the bank or account you want the money deposited into. Type in the amount of Bitcoin you want to deposit and click sell Bitcoin. That's it.

You have successfully traded your cryptocurrency for Bitcoin and exchanged Bitcoin for USD.

GETTING YOUR HARDWARE AND BUILDING YOUR RIG

For this chapter, we are going to get into the nitty-gritty of building your rig and mining. For the purpose of this chapter, we will look at building and Ethereum rig. This will go through sourcing your equipment as well as putting it together. This could take you up to a week to accomplish. You also have the option of buying a cloud mining contract through Genesis Mining or Hashflare if you are not interested in buying mining equipment.

Sourcing Equipment

You need to get a hold of a lot of components, and the costs can stack up.

1. Motherboard

The brain of your computer, the motherboard is what everything is built into and the base of your rig. The main thing you need to look at for your motherboard is how many GPU slots it has because this will determine how many GPU's or graphics cards it can hold, which is what determines your hashing power. If the motherboard has 3 PCI Express slots, then you will be able to fit 3 x Radeon HD 7950 and have a hash rate of 20 MH/s each, which will give you a complete hashing power of 60 MH/s. The PCI Express slot is the connection spot on your motherboard. They are typically white, but they may be beige. There are other types of slots but for the most part GPU's work on PCI.

2. Graphics card

Now you pick your GPUs. There are some graphics cards out there that will cost you an arm and a leg, but they have horrible hashing power. Then there are others that are more reasonably priced and have more power. You basically need to find a balance between the power you are looking for and how much you are willing to spend. The important thing is that you pick an efficient GPU. You can purchase refurbished GPUs from reputable sites like GPU shack. You have to be careful though; there are a lot of second-hand cards that have problems that you won't discover until you plug them in.

There is one common issue that you can have with your motherboard and graphics card. You may find that they don't all fit together perfectly because of how the PCI Express slots are spaced on the motherboard. Fear not, you can get a riser which works like an extension cable for the slot. There are some graphics cards that are bulky, so be careful when you are choosing your card.

3. Hard drive

The hard drive is needed for you to store your operating system and the mining software on. You can use a standard SSD drive. The size you need will depend on what you want to do when you are mining. If you are interested in downloading the complete blockchain, then you need to consider how large the blockchain will become and the time you need to spend on it. If you plan on mining Ethereum as part of a pool than you won't have to store the blockchain and you will be able to get a smaller SSD drive.

4. RAM

This is one of the most basic components of all computers and works as a scratchpad for writing down calculations and being able to call that information up quickly on your computer. 4GB should be big enough.

5. PSU

You can get power supply units in several different sizes, and this can cause problems for some when they are trying to figure out the size they need. You should add up your GPU's power consumption and all of your other components, and then make sure that that the power supply has a bigger power supply. If you are using two GPUs that use 220 watts and your other components take up another 250 watts, then you can use a 750-watt power supply unit because the complete amount of power you need is only 690 watts. If you plan on building a "mega rig" that contains six GPU's, you may find that it is more cost efficient to use two different power supplies. Two 750 watt PSU at the cost of $100 a piece is better than $300 for a single 1500 watt PSU.

6. A case

This can prove to be fairly difficult choice because it will depend on your GPU's, as well as whether or not you are using risers. You need to make sure you don't have components sitting on top of one another as this is a fire hazard. You can choose to leave your system open air; you can build a case for it yourself to give it a little personalization. You can also choose to buy an off the shelf rig from a few providers. They can take awhile to get to you, but all of the hard work is done.

gpuShack.com is a great website to source your components. They offer group packages, which can make it cheaper for you.

Putting Your Rig Together

Like I said earlier, you need to make sure that your power supply will be able to handle your graphics cards, and then you also have risers that will give you the chance to place extra GPU's in safe place. All of the connections need to be plugged in correctly and that everything is held together.

A word of advice on positioning, GPU's can become hot, especially if they are overclocked, so you need to make sure you get the best bang for your buck. You also need to make sure that your rig is placed in a well-ventilated area so that you don't risk it overheating.

Once your rig is turned on, you will want to make sure that all of the software you need for mining is on your rig.

Software

The first thing you have to do is to install an operating system onto your rig. For people who are more technically minded, you can use Linux Ubuntu, but for most people, Windows is the best choice because it automates installing drivers so that all of the components talk correctly to each other. The best part of Ubuntu, though, is it provides a lot of options and its free.

You can also choose to download EthOs, which is an APP that was specifically designed for Ethereum mining. This is the perfect way a specific mining system for your GPU's and rigs to manage all of them.

After you have downloaded your operating system onto your rig, there are two ways that you are able to start mining:

- Solo mining – this type of mining means that it is you against everybody else. If you create the correct hash, then you will get the block reward. If you have a rig of 60 MH/s and a hashing power of 1.2 GH, you probably won't see much ether. You will also need to download the blockchain.
- Pool mining – this type of mining requires you to team up with other miners to lower the volatility of returns. This could mean that you get five ether every five days, or you get an ether every single day. The best thing about this is that you get a continued stream of ether and you won't need to download the complete blockchain.

Mining Ethereum

You should now have a pretty good understanding of how mining works, so you are probably itching to get started mining yourself. As a little refresher, mining is what holds the 'decentralized app store' together by making sure that there is a consensus for every change to the applications that are running on the network.

Take, for example, the online notebook that is described in "What is Ethereum?" The network was unable to reach a consensus about the notebook's state, as if a note was deleted or added, without computational power to process through the changes.

Miners allow their computers to go crazy to solve cryptographic puzzles in an attempt to get ether, and they need to try a large number of computational problems until somebody can unlock a new asset batch.

A very interesting part of an open blockchain is that, theoretically, anybody can set their computers to only focus on these puzzles as a way for them to win the mining rewards. The problem is that mining on these public blockchains will eventually require even more power over a period of time as more people begin investing in better hardware.

It is now very unlikely for those that are mining with low-powered setups for them to win, but it is still a pretty decent past-time for enthusiast and hobbyists.

As you learned earlier, you need a rig that is solely used for mining. You can choose from GPUs and CPUs, as you know. GPUs will provide you with a better has rated. GPUs are the only option for a person that is interested in mining ether.

Getting your GPU together can be quite complex, so make sure that you get others advice, and don't rely only on this book. Other people may have good advice on the most profitable choices based on hash rate, initial expense, and power consumption.

You can also find mining profitability calculators that will show how much you may be able to earn given your hash rate when set against the electricity cost and setup.

After you have set up your rig, and have taken care of your hardware, you need to get your software ready. Miners will need to install a client that can connect to the network. People who are familiar with a command line can choose to install geth, which will run an ethereum node written in 'Go,' a scripting language.

After you have your software downloaded, your node will be able to talk with other nodes, which will connect it to the Ethereum network. Besides the fact that it can be used to mine ether, it will give you the interface to deploy smart contracts and send transactions with a command line.

Testing

You can also choose to mine 'test' ether on a private network so that you can experiment with the decentralized applications or smart contracts. Mining on a test network won't require fancy hardware on your part. All you will need is a home computer with geth or some other client installed. Minting fake ether isn't going to be all that lucrative.

Install Ethminer

If you are planning on mining real ether, you need to install mining software. After you have downloaded a client and your node has become a part of the network, you will then need to download Ethminer. You will need to find the right download version for your operating system.

After this has been installed, your node will start to play a part in staking your place in the Ethereum network.

Join a Mining Pool

You probably won't be that successful as a sole miner of ether. This is why there are miner pools. Miners 'pool' their computational power together to create a mining pool. This will improve the chances of solving the puzzles and getting a reward for everybody involved in the pool. They will then split their profits proportional to the amount of power the miner contributed.

There are a lot of different factors that are involved in jumping into a mining pool. Every pool probably won't stay around for forever, and the computational power of all of these pools change constantly, so there are a few factors that you need to consider before you decide to join one.

One important thing that you need to remember is that mining pools have different types of payout structures. A mining pool will a signup process on their website so that miners are able to connect with the pool and then start mining.

You have to remember the world of mining is a whirlwind of change. The tools that you learn today could disappear next year, and there are mining pools that may fall away while others are created, so you have to keep an eye out for industry shifts.

Mining Bitcoin

Mining Bitcoin works pretty much the same as mining Ethereum. You will need to have you mining rig set up and ready to go. For the most part, you will probably need to make sure you get an ASIC if you are interested in mining Bitcoin. Otherwise, you probably aren't going to see much in return. You will then need to download the mining software. There are a lot of programs that you can use for Bitcoin, but the most popular choices are BFGminer and CGminer which work as command line programs.

If you want the ease of use that you can get with a GUI, then you may want to download EasyMiner, which works as a click and go

Android/Windows/Linux program.

After you have everything ready to start mining, it is best that you join a Bitcoin mining pool. Without using a mining pool, you might be stuck mining Bitcoins for years and never earn a single one. It's a lot easier to share the work and then split the reward a group of miners.

If you want a fully decentralized pool, you can use p2pool. As of right now, the following pools fully validate block using the Bitcoin core 0.9.5 or later:

- Slush Pool
- Eligius
- CK Pool
- BitMinter

No matter what coin you are mining, you will need to make sure that you have a wallet for your coins to be deposited in. Above all else, make sure that you stay up to date on all the current Bitcoin news. This is important for your profits.

Writing Script

If you are planning on using cpuminer, you will need to know how to set up your parameters for mining. It's easier to create a one-line script, called a batch file in Windows, to launch your miner with the right instructions.

For this you will need:

- Worker password
- Worker number or name
- Mining pool username
- Port number for the server

- Stratum URL for the mining pool server
- Full path to the directory where your program is stored

You will then need to open Notepad or your text editor of choice. You should not ever use a word processor like MS word. Next, you will need to type in the script. This method assumes that you are trying to mine a currency that uses the scrypt algorithm.

Start "path" minerd.exe – url URL:PORT –a scrypt - - userpass USERNAME.WORKER:PASSWORD

When you type in the above details, you should get the following:

Start "C:|cpu-miner-pooler" minerd.exe –url stratum+tcp://pool.d2.cc:3333 –a scrypt – userpass username.1:x

You will then need to save this file with a ".bat" extension. After you have saved the batch file, double-click it to activate your new miner program. The mining pool is probably going to have a web-based interface. After a few minutes, the website should start to show that you are actively mining.

GPU Miner Setup

For those that you interested in mining with GPUs, which would be anybody that creates a mining rig, you should use the cgminer program. Versions of cgminer past 3.72, do not support scrypt mining, this means that you shouldn't just download the latest version. You will need to find the version that offers everything you need.

This setup is assuming you are using Windows. If you are using OS X or Linus, the command line arguments are going to be the same.

You need to extract the software into a folder that you are able to find easily. You now need to make sure that your graphics drivers are up to date. You then need to press the Windows key with the "R" key. Then type in the "cmd," and then select enter. This will give you a command terminal. You can then use the "cd" command to switch the directory to the one that has the cgminer file.

Type in "cgminer.exe –n." This will give you the list of the recognized devices on your PC. If it can detect your graphics card, then you can go to the next step. If it does not detect your graphics card, then you need to research the steps required for properly setting up your graphics card. Then make sure you have the information for your mining pool. This is the same information that you needed for the CPU setup.

Now you need to create a batch file so that you can start your cgminer correctly.

Start "path" cgminer – scrypt –o URL:PORT –u USERNAME.WORKER –p PASSWORD

Now you have your chosen mining software set up, you will start to see statistics scrolling through the command line. If you have cgminer, you are going to get more info than that with cpuminer. With the cgminer, you will see information about the mining hardware, mining pool, and currency. If you are using cpuminer, you are only going to see information about the blocks that your computer has solved, and your hashing speed.

The great thing for people who have a PC with dedicated graphics cards, you can run cgminer and cpuminer together. To this, you will add a "-threads n" argument into the minerd command. In this, the "n" stands for the number of CPU cores that you want to employ.

You need to make sure that you leave a few of these cores free to work your GPUs. If you set minerd to use all of your CPU cores your CPU will be too busy to send data to the GPU. If you have a quad core CPU, then you should set the argument to "2" or "3."

When you mine with CPU and GPU, you will be able to see how much better GPUs are when it comes to mining. Look at the hash rates in your terminal window for your programs, and you will likely see at least five times the difference.

DUMP FOR DOLLARS, OR KEEP THE CRYPTOCURRENCY

One of the biggest questions people will ask is which cryptocurrency they should buy. Another commonality for the beginner is that they don't spend most of their day listing to the options of cryptocurrency experts and personalities, doing extensive research, and analyzing the market.

Even if there is some seemingly knowledgeable and trustworthy "expert" that tells you that you need to invest in cryptocurrency A or B, a beginner doesn't have the business experience or technical skills to evaluate if this is or isn't a person that you can trust.

One thing is for certain; beginners aren't interested in getting into a coin that has huge volatility and an unknown future. This means that it only makes sense for them to get into coins that are built on solid tech, a strong team, and solid business plan.

When you have mined or bought cryptocurrencies, there are few things to look at so that you can figure out if you should keep it or sell it for dollars:

- Is there a highly reputable team backing this coin?
- How active are they in improving and maintaining their coin?
- Are they actively communicating with their investors?
- Is the coin blockchain based?
- How many coins are in circulation and what is a total number of coins?
- How much are they worth?

- How many coins were premined and are you able to mine them?
- How many exchanges have these coins?

Now that we have gone through some important steps you should take, let's look at the coins that I would suggest holding onto. This should not be used as investment advice; it's only an opinion.

Steem

This cryptocurrency is used on the social media blogging platform Steemit. They also have a Steem dollar, which means they have two cryptocurrencies. The Steem dollar will only ever be worth a dollar, whereas Steem's value will depend on the market.

I believe most of its value comes from Steemit. Platforms such as Twitter and Facebook aren't incentivized. You have a greater chance having to pay them to use the site, than making money from it. Steemit gives you the chance to make Steem dollars and Steem by posting quality content. You can blog for money on Steemit, but the upvotes you receive for your content is what determines the amount you earn.

You can also power up your Steem by using Steem power. Steem power is what decided the worth of your vote. If you were to have 1,000 Steem power, your upvote would be worth 20 cents. But, if you have 500,000 Steem power, the upvote would worth $100. Basically, you are encouraged to spend money on Steemit.

If you want to withdraw money, you will have to wait three months to power down. This keeps people from being able to move money away from Steemit, which keeps the value of Steemit.

Ark

Ark is known for their SmartBridge technology. This technology allows people to link different blockchains together through their bridging method. Think about linking together the Lisk blockchain and Ethereum blockchain.

Their team is also pretty competent. Some of them have helped develop Crypti and Lisk. They also have other amazing features like an interplanetary file system, physical card system, optional privacy, and fast transaction speed. It's a coin that looks to be on the rise.

Siacoin

Currently ranked in the top 40 of cryptocurrencies, Siacoin has a market cap of just higher than $200 million. 28 billion Siacoins are in circulation, and it will quickly reach its cap of over 40 billion.

The value of this coin comes from the fact that it is one of the few coins that have a product. It has a decentralized storage space that has better safeguards from hackers when compared to the other mainstream cloud services. It will likely be able to compete with cloud storages provided by Google Drive, Microsoft Dropbox, and Amazon S3, at a lower price. The price for their service will be affected by the market forces.

Paying less for cloud storage is what Siacoin hopes to achieve. You need 2,000 Siacoins to be able to use this service. You will also get the chance to rent out space to others. Since the coins and storage are limited, the value will definitely increase.

It does have some competition with Storj and Maid Safe coin.

Monero

Monero has better anonymity than Bitcoin, which is the reason why its worth was able to go up from $50 to $125 in only a few days. The biggest reason to keep Monero is the user anonymity. There are a lot of sophisticated and intricate methods to create this privacy. It can be broken down into several different methods.

It makes use of a stealth address. If you trade with other types of coins, you will probably see a destination address, and this means that others are able to track you. Monero only displays cryptographic hashes for the destination address. The recipient and sender are the only two people who can read the hash.

They make use of separate transaction units. Let's say you send 100 XMR; it will be delivered to the recipient in separate sums of 30, 20, and 50 XMR. They are each recoded separately, making it harder to track. They also use ring signatures to mix up the transactions and to make anonymity possible.

Ethereum

Ethereum is seen as the best alternative to Bitcoin, and you can see this in its price. In September 2017 it traded at $380. The biggest success for Ethereum is its introduction of the Ethereum network. It made programming on blockchain a lot easier, and this is the reason why there are so many popular coins that are based on this network. Golem and OmiseGo are two great options.

Smart contracts are another reason why Ethereum is so popular. Bitcoin's smart contract consists of sending and receiving coins. Ethereum's smart contracts take things to a whole new level. It gives people the change to manage agreements and makes sure that a payment is made when it is supposed to be.

OmiseGo

This coin is based in Thailand and provides Southeast Asia Stripe-like payment features. The coin is based on Ethereum's network, and it provides the user with real-time payment services and value exchange across jurisdictions. It also lets a user exchange both cryptocurrencies and fiat currencies.

Holders of OMG will be able to make money through transaction fees. The more transactions there are, the more money a holder will make. Because of this, the price of OMG will rise.

The best part of OMG is their financial transaction, which includes business to business commerce, payments, loyalty programs, remittances, and more. They are also done in an inexpensive way.

Iota

As of right now, Iota is the only coin that isn't based on blockchain. It has a new data transfer and transactional settlement layer for the internet of things. The coin is based on a distributed ledger known as Tangle, and its goal is to overcome the problems of blockchain.

Theoretically, it has no transaction fees, unlimited transaction rate, and no miners. This means that it does not have a scalability problem. It also gives people the chance to use small nanopayments. You are also unable to split a coin.

So What Should You Do?

With digital currencies, nobody can be for certain. There is always a risk when getting involved in cryptocurrencies, especially if you choose to invest in them. There is a chance that a $50 coin could end up being worth 50 cents the next day. The listed coins above have a good chance of continuing to rise in value, which means it is a good idea to hold them. As far as selling them for a fiat currency, that comes down to you. Keep an eye on the market to see how things are looking for the coin, and then decide whether you would be better off keeping it or selling it.

FUTURE OF CRYPTOCURRENCY

Cryptocurrencies were able to make the jump from an academic concept to reality when Bitcoin was launched in 2009. Bitcoin continued to attract more followers in the subsequent years, and in 2013 in caught the attention of the media and investors when it hit a record of $266 per Bitcoin. Bitcoin has carried a market value of more than two billion dollars at its peak, but then it experienced a 50% plunge, which caused a raging debate about the cryptocurrencies future. Are these currencies going to supplant conventional currencies and become as universal as the euro and dollar? Or are they more of a passing fad that will fade away in a few years? Bitcoin seems to hold the answer.

The Current Standard

The decentralized nature of Bitcoin makes it free from interference or manipulation of the government. It also means that there isn't a central authority to make sure that everything runs smoothly or anything to back its value. The digital coins are created through mining that requires computers to figure out complex algorithms. The current rate of creation is 25 Bitcoins every ten minutes, and the amount is capped at 21 million, which is expected to be reached in the year 2140.

This is what makes Bitcoin so different from the regular fiat currencies, which has the backing of its government. Fiat currencies are centralized and supervised by a central bank of a nation. While a bank is in control of how much of the currency is given in accordance with the policy, there isn't an upper limit to how much can be issued. Deposits are typically insured against any failures of the bank by a governing body. Bitcoin does not have any of these support mechanisms. Bitcoin's value is completely dependent on what investors will pay for it at any given time. If a Bitcoin exchange were to fold up, the people who have Bitcoin balances have no way of getting them back.

The transaction anonymity and decentralization benefits of Bitcoin have also made it a favorite payment for a lot of illegal activity, which include weapons procurement, smuggling, drug peddling, and money laundering. This has caused it to attract the attention of government agencies like the SEC, Financial Crimes Enforcement Network, Department of Homeland Security, and FBI. The FinCEN issued new rules in March 2013 that defined these virtual administrators and exchanges as money service businesses, which brought them within the scope of government regulation. In May of the same year, the DHS froze a Mt. Gox account that was held at Wells Fargo, saying that anti-money laundering laws were broke. Then on August, 22 emerging payment companies were issued subpoenas by New York's Department of Financial Services. Many of these companies handled Bitcoin. The subpoenas looked to find out the measures they were taking to prevent money laundering, and how they would ensure consumer protection.

Bitcoin Alternatives

Despite the issues it has had, Bitcoin's growing visibility and success has caused several companies to unveil alternative coins, like:

- Litecoin – presently, this altcoin is seen as Bitcoin's biggest rival. It was created to process small transactions faster. Unlike the computer horsepower you need for Bitcoin, Litecoin can be mined using a normal computer. Litecoin has a max of 84 million coins, which is four times more than Bitcoin's limit.

- Ripple – OpenCoin launched Ripple. The payment mechanism for Ripple allows for funds transfers in any currency to a Ripple use in a matter of seconds, which is a big difference to Bitcoin's ten-minute confirmation.

- MintChip — Unlike most other altcoins, MintChip was created by a government institution. This currency is a smart card that has an electronic value, and it can be transferred between chips. MintChip does not require any personal identification, but it is backed by the Canadian dollar.

The Future

The current limitations that cryptocurrencies face, like a person's digital fortune being erased by a crash, or a virtual vault being ransacked by a hacker, could be overcome in time with new advances. What's harder to fix is the paradox of cryptocurrencies: the more they grow in popularity, the more government regulation and scrutiny that will attract, which will eventually erode the fundamental purpose.

While there may be a growing number of merchants who accept these cryptocurrencies, they are still a minority. For them to become used more widely, they will need to gain widespread acceptance among their users. Their complexity, when compared to other currencies, will probably deter people, except for those that are technically adept.

A cryptocurrency that is looking to become part of the mainstream financial world will have to satisfy a wide array of criteria. It will need to be mathematically complex to fight off hackers, but easy enough for the regular consumer to understand. It should be decentralized, but have enough safeguards for consumer protection. It also needs to keep user anonymity without it being used for money laundering, tax evasion, and other illegal activities.

Since all of this is a lot to satisfy, there is a chance that some of the popular cryptocurrencies out there, in a few years, could develop attributes that lie between today's cryptocurrencies and regulated fiat currencies. While this seems like a remote possibility, there is very little doubt that Bitcoin's success in handling these challenges may determine the outlook for altcoins in the coming years.

CONCLUSION

Thanks for making it through to the end of *Cryptocurrency Mining*. Let's hope it was informative and able to provide you with all of the tools you need to achieve your goals.

The next step is to use the information you have learned to help you start your mining rig. Mining cryptocurrencies can be very rewarding if you do things the right way. Continue to research more, and become an amazing miner.

Finally, if you found this book useful in any way, a review on Amazon is always appreciated!

www.ingramcontent.com/pod-product-compliance
Lightning Source LLC
Chambersburg PA
CBHW070200230526
45471CB00002B/756